LETTING GO OF
PERFECTION

Embracing the Mess and Finding Your Balance

Sheri Poyant
BS, M.A.T.

Published by

Business Growth Advisors

SYDNEY, AUSTRALIA

MDA Publishing
Higginbotham Rd
Gladesville, NSW, 2111
Australia

Book Layout © 2021

Letting Go of Perfection -- 1st ed.
ISBN 978-0-6450942-6-8

Forward

Sheri is one of the most loving, gracious and kind people I know. She gives with everything she is, and her heart truly shows in all she does.

This book will move you in such a way that you will never be the same. You will immediately be a changed person because of what Sheri shares of her own journey in these pages.

She knows firsthand how perfectionism destroys people and relationships from the inside out, and her heart is focused on making sure she can shorten other peoples' learning curves as it relates to releasing it.

Sit back, grab some tea and enjoy what you are about to experience. It was made with love for you.

Martha Krejci
Mother, Wife, Speaker, Author, Creative Disrupter, and CEO Martha K Media Group

Introduction

In this book, I am giving you permission to let go of perfection. Perfection can be such a destructive force, it can be debilitating, creating anxiety and frustration. It can get in the way of you living the life that you want to live. Throughout this book, I am going to share with you how I let go of perfection, which has helped me to lead a much more fulfilling life.

When you let go of perfection, you will uncover ways to be more joyful and free. You will be able to truly live out your life's purpose. You won't be tied down to unhelpful thoughts, or ideas of how things SHOULD be, or what other people think. Rather, you will learn to be more present so you can enjoy the life that you have.

In this book, I will teach you how to let go of perfection with three key ideas. First, we are going to focus on awareness- in order to make changes, we need to first understand what drives us. We are going to "switch on the light". We will begin to understand why you are a perfectionist, and what drives you. We will take a look at past patterns.

Once we have switched on that light, we are going to look at how perfection has affected your life- your work, your relationships, your emotions, and physical health. We will explore how we as perfectionists build a value system around being perfect. We will explore the price of perfection, and what you can focus on to move forward toward a more purpose driven life. For me, the price of perfection was strained relationships, feelings of despair and anxiety, as well as developing autoimmune issues, that were at times, debilitating. Depression set in when I was not able to handle all that was thrown at me in life, and I became overwhelmed with sadness.

And lastly, I am going to share with you how you too can become a recovering perfectionist.

I am going to teach you about how to let go, and the first step of that is about forgiveness; forgiveness of yourself, and others. We are going to dive into repairing relationships, and how to put things in place that will help you to no longer be a victim to perfectionism. I will share my 7 key daily practices that will help you to stay present, happy and free.

You are reading this book for a reason- maybe you saw yourself in the title or the cover. You are realizing that if you continue on this path of perfectionism, you will not fully get to enjoy life- your family, your faith, your spouse, your work, your children. I was stuck in this cycle of anxiety, depression, and illness. Kind of like a goldfish in a fishbowl, just getting stuck in the same place, and going around and around in a bowl.

Here's a really cool thing. When you become aware of how perfection has driven you, and understand its toll on your health and relationships, and then put into practice the 7 principles, you will get to be really present in your life and enjoy every wonderful moment. My wish for you is that this book helps you to let go of perfection and start living a life that you really will enjoy.

XO,
Sheri

Excellence is not the same as perfection.

ABOUT THE AUTHOR

Sheri Poyant is an author, entrepreneur, and health, life and business coach. She lives in Rhode Island with her husband Matt, her son Andrew, and their Golden Retriever Princess Kate.

Sheri loves running, and she is currently training for her third marathon. She enjoys her Saturday morning runs with her running group.

Sheri also loves Disney World, and enjoys vacationing there with her family each year- her first marathon was in all four amusement parks in Walt Disney World!

Sheri and her husband Matt created a movement called #52firstdates, encouraging other couples to focus on their marriage, by dating each other once a week. They are enjoying their weekly dates, and spending time together.

Sheri loves watching her son play basketball, drinking coffee on the front porch, gardening, and family walks with Kate. Her favorite day of the week is Sunday, which includes spending time together with her sister Kelly and her family.

Sheri's passion is coaching women, and helping them to find balance in health, relationships and career. Her mission is to impact one million families, helping them to live differently, to have a clear purpose, and a plan to make their dreams a reality.

ACKNOWLEDGEMENTS

They say it takes a village to raise a child. It also takes a village of support to get through depression, anxiety and illness.

I have to start by thanking my husband and best friend Matt for his love, support and encouragement. He is my rock, and truly the "Perfect" Poyant husband, in every way. He supports me in everything I do. I love you always, Matty!

I am so thankful for my son Andrew –for his big heart, love, and understanding when I was suffering. Thanks bud for being the sunshine on my darkest days, and always. I am so proud of the amazing young man you have become.

I would have not gotten through the difficult times in my life without the love and encouragement from my sister Kelly. Kel, I love you, Howie, and Bella so much.

To the women in my life who stepped in when I needed a mom- Anita, June, Pat and Doris, I am forever grateful for your love and kindness.

Thank you to my friends who have been by my side through the sadness and happiness. I am beyond blessed to have the most amazing group of women in my life!

Thank you so much Brett for helping to pull this story out of me, from the depths of my soul, where it was hidden away. You saw something in me when we were talking about perfection, and I am hopeful that this book helps release the need for perfectionism in other women.

Thank you to my coach and mentor Martha. You have inspired me to share my story, and to live in service, helping other women to rise up out of the darkness. Your guidance, faith in me, and encouragement has meant the world to me.

Lastly, to my mom and dad, I hope that I have made you proud being imperfectly me, and that you are smiling down on me- I miss you both and love you always.

I am forever grateful, XO Sheri

TABLE OF CONTENTS

SECTION 1

LETTING GO OF PERFECTION

CHAPTER ONE

PERFECTION IS OVERRATED

My perfectionism started affecting my health way back in 1999. I was student teaching and working towards my master's degree. I was also taking a graduate course, and I was chosen to create a special portfolio pilot project of my teaching. This extra work put a lot of pressure on me. I wanted to do really well, and I wanted to earn a 4.0 and the distinguish of Honors in Student Teaching. I was determined to be the best student and teacher I could be, to make my parents, my husband, and my professor proud.

One weekend during that semester, I worked 20 hours on a project. I stopped only to eat and sleep. I went to my student teaching placement on Monday. I remember standing in front of the classroom, and the strangest sensation came over me. I had this strange feeling in my nose, then a pain came from the back of my head, to the front of my face. It felt like someone was sticking a knife into my face. I was rushed to the hospital, and they tested me for everything from MS to meningitis.

I was finally diagnosed with trigeminal neuralgia, which is nicknamed the "suicide" headache, because the pain is so unbearable that it can make you want to end it any way possible. I was put on all kinds of medications. Then I started getting migraines, and a range of other illnesses from the stress. Somehow, through all of this illness, I managed to finish the semester with that 4.0, the portfolio completed, and I received the distinguished Honors in Student Teaching.

But at what price? I think about it now. What did that project really mean to me? The portfolio was used by the college as a pilot for a new graduation requirement. A copy is at the college (at least it was!), and today my copy sits in my closet. The cost of that semester, trying to be the perfect teacher and student, was my health. I didn't realize it then, but I should have. The big clue was that the headaches stopped when I finished my teaching assignment.

Some years later, a light bulb went off, and I realized at that time I was striving for perfection and putting all kinds of stress on myself that was causing my physical illnesses. Today I teach college students, and I try to instill in my students that grades aren't everything. It is important to work hard, and to hand in work on time. But I truly believe that the process of learning is more important than getting everything perfect, because when you are striving for perfection, you can lose track of what is most important- learning and then being able to apply what you learn.

This is actually what I teach about in early childhood education courses, the process and the journey of learning is what is important when teaching young children. I also try to instill this belief in my teenage son. Instead of asking him what his grades are, I ask, "What is something new you learned?" and "How can you use it?" "What did you learn that was interesting?"

When I was in graduate school, I was striving to be the best graduate student in the program, to get a 4.0 grade point average, and get Honors in Student Teaching. And you know what? That didn't matter at all when I went to get a teaching job. What mattered was how I could apply what I learned. But I had this sense that if I got perfect grades, and had everyone's praises, that it was worth it.

As I look back, honestly, getting sick wasn't worth it. Not at all! At the time, I was so focused on getting a 4.0 that I missed out on enjoying other things that were happening in my life, like buying our first house. I was so focused on school that anything else I had to do was a distraction. It is a hard lesson that I have learned- when I was so focused on doing well, and would not accept anything less, I constantly worried. When you are worrying all the time, you can miss out on what is happening in the present.

At the time, I missed out on what was happening around me. I was so sick from the stress that I could not enjoy the other fun and exciting things in my life. Over the years, I have learned how important it is to stay in the present. This change of heart (and mind!) did not happen all of a sudden; it happened over time, as I learned from my past mistakes.

One of the biggest lessons I learned as I reflect on my past is this.

Perfection is overrated; happy is where it is at.

Learn to Embrace the Mess

In order to let go, I let messy in. Yes, I learned to embrace the mess that life can sometimes throw at me. That doesn't mean I am a total mess, (at least I don't think so!). It means that it is okay if my house isn't perfectly clean (no one ever died from a little dirt!). It is okay if there are tumble weeds of fur from my Golden Retriever in the corners of the room (advice- don't get dark hardwood floors if you plan on having a Golden!). It is okay if the laundry is not always done on time.

By letting those things go a little bit, I have been able to be more present in my life, with my husband, my son, and with my work. I can have FUN! I can live out my purpose, which is helping other women to find balance in their lives, which brings even more joy and happiness to my life.

The Webster's Dictionary definition of perfection is "the quality or state of being perfect: such as freedom from fault or defect, flawlessness, or a state of being saintly." When you see this definition in black and white, it can kind of make you stop and think, wow- what made me think I could be, or should be, flawless?

When you're focused on being a perfect being, your thoughts are rarely in the present. You're either thinking into the future and worrying about things which can cause anxiety, or you are thinking back to things in the past you feel guilty about, which can contribute to depression. When attempting to stay in the present moment and practicing mindfulness, you have the opportunity to find joy and happiness in what is happening around you, instead of worrying about what is going to happen tomorrow, or next week.

Letting go of trying to be perfect gives you the freedom to live your life. Giving yourself permission to let go allows you to LIVE out your true purpose, whatever that is. One thing I know for sure is if you're always striving for perfection, it may hold you back from getting to where you want to go, because it is holding you back from letting go. Many perfectionists never finish projects or meet their goals, because they get in their own way-they are so consumed by the outcome being the way they imagine it, that anything less is not good enough. Then, when things are not finished the way they imagined or dreamed, that can also create feelings of inadequacy, sadness, and fear of not being good enough.

I have read studies that show perfectionism can cause things like anxiety, depression, autoimmune disease, and other stress related illnesses. It is real, and I know that personally from my own experience, but it can be managed if we have the right tools in our toolbox.

"You are enough.
You are so enough it is
unbelievable how
enough you are."
-Sierra Bogges

CHAPTER TWO

THE ILLUSION OF PERFECTION

As stated previously, perfection means to be flawless. Who among us is flawless? There honestly is no perfection here on earth, and when you're always striving for perfection, whether it is creating the perfect meal, hosting the perfect holiday, having the perfectly decorated house for Christmas, or doing your job perfectly, when you don't get that, when things are messy and don't go your way, you start to internalize it, and that can cause stress in your body. That stress can manifest itself into frustration, anger, anxiety and sadness, that can then show up as illness.

When there has been stress in my life, I always had this irrational thought process, that if everything looks perfect on the outside, I can handle it. Have you ever felt that way? If the house is perfectly clean, or your family is all dressed nicely, or you make beautiful cupcakes, it makes you look (and maybe feel) like you are in control. It is what I call the "facade of perfection".

But here is what happens- it becomes a vicious cycle, you want everything perfect, so you become totally focused on making things perfect, which stresses you out. The stress starts to take over, and you start to internalize it. For me, the more I tried to control things, the more it felt like things were spinning out of control. Everything looks perfect and put together on the outside, but the stress of living that way caused a physical and mental decline in me. I ended up sick with autoimmune issues, allergies, asthma, hives, migraines, and debilitating fatigue.

When I said enough is enough, and I started to let go of perfection, of trying to be the perfect mom, the perfect wife, the perfect teacher, the perfect everything, and just be myself, I felt much better. I became more comfortable in my own skin, and became happier, more relaxed, and (I think!) more fun to be around.

When I was able to let go of worrying about what other people thought of me, of worry about what everyone else was doing, and what I thought they expected of me, the stress started to dissipate. When I stopped doing things to please others, trying to live up to other people's expectations, and trying to look like I had it all together (when I clearly didn't), I was able to truly find happiness, as I let the messy in.

The Desire to Please at Any Cost

When you are a perfectionist, many times that desire for perfection can come from trying to please others, or for the praise that they give you for a job well done. That praise strokes the ego and makes you feel like you are valued and special. Your ego thrives on praise and compliments. You care about what other people think of you. You may have learned this in school at an early age, be good and you will be praised. Raise your hand, follow the rules and your teacher will like you. You may have learned this from your parents. You may have thought from your experiences that if you are not perfect, you are not loveable.

I learned in kindergarten how being a "good little girl" would earn me praise from my teacher and my parents. I loved my kindergarten teacher. She had long hair down her back, and she was so sweet to all of the children. Kindergarten was my first experience at school, away from my mom, and I loved every minute.

I still remember coming home from school with my first report card. There were little comments from my teacher on it, and I remember my parent's faces lighting up when they saw it. My teacher called me "a little doll" and my parents were so proud.

I learned that I could get positive attention by doing well in school- I relished my parents praise, and I loved when they were proud of me. I wanted to make them both happy. I was the oldest of three girls, and I saw quickly that this was my role, I was the one that the teachers loved, the one who sat with her hands folded, working hard on her work, and always trying her best.

I was actually scared to get in trouble- I didn't want to disappoint my parents. I had straight A's right through fourth grade. In fifth grade I came home with a B on my report card, and I was terrified about what my parents would say. I had expectations within my family of this façade of perfection.

As I look back, I believe that school, along with my parent's expectations, unintentionally shaped me, and the pressures that I put on myself. My mom strived to be a perfect mom- and she was an amazing mom. She had cookies baked for us when we got home from school. She volunteered at our schools, she drove us to the bus stop when it was raining, and she made every holiday so special. But my mom also seemed to have a need for perfection. She was a stay-at-home mom, and my guess is that, like me, when I was a stay-at-home mom, she felt like it was her job. She wanted to make a nice home for us kids and for our dad. When you are a stay-at-home mom, sometimes you have guilt that you are not contributing financially (at least I did), so you overcompensate in other ways.

When I think of my mom back then, she did not seem happy all the time. She was stressed, and in turn it made me stressed. We had some difficult rules as kids- we couldn't play in our bedrooms, and we weren't allowed to sit on our beds because we might wrinkle the bedspread. I remember my mom constantly cleaning and seeming to be angry about it. It's funny, we as parents can do so many fun and positive things for our kids, but what tends to stick in kids' memories is the stressful and hard stuff. It is a hard lesson that I learned, and as a parent I have worked hard to not be that stressed out mom for my son. Have I been totally stressed at times? Yes! But I have made conscious choices to let things go, and not sweat the small stuff with my son. I don't want to repeat the cycle with him.

I am perfectly
imperfect.

CHAPTER THREE

THE "AH-HA" MOMENTS

So, you are reading this and maybe you are thinking, hey, this totally sounds like me. The light bulb, or awareness, is switching on for you. In order to let go of perfectionism, you first need to develop an awareness that you are a perfectionist. To understand you are a perfectionist, you have to dive deep into your past thoughts, habits, and actions.

You may want to start with asking yourself a few questions. If you feel stressed all the time, start to examine why you are getting stressed:

- What is stressing you out?

- Are you mad at your kids all the time?
- Are you frustrated because the dishes are left in the sink?
- Are you angry because the laundry is not done?
- Are you snapping at everybody?

Take some time to reflect on your answers, so you can start to develop a deeper understanding of what is actually going on with you.

Some questions that I really needed to spend time reflecting on was:

- What are my values?
- Why do I need to control everything?
- Why do I want things to look, or be perfect?
- Does that reflect on who I am, deep inside?
- Why do I care what other people think of me?
- Why do I seek their praise?
- What does it matter what car I drive, or what clothes I wear?

My son recently said to me that it is hard to be different, but he does it anyway (as he got in my car with flip flops and wild socks on his feet that did not match his outfit!).

I learned long ago to let him decide what he wants to wear- if he doesn't match, and he doesn't care, what difference does it make? Why do we care what others think of us?

Have you heard the expression Insta-perfect? Coaches everywhere sell filters and courses to teach business owners and influencers how to create the perfect Instagram feed. Go ahead and take a look at some Instagram influencers and you will most likely notice that all of their pictures are "perfect"- kids happily smiling or helping them do their videos, quotes positioned in the perfect spot in their feed and all the photos have the same beautiful filter. I honestly started not posting on Instagram because of the pressures of the "perfect feed."

It was becoming so stressful for me-and frankly too much work, until I realized that if I don't post there, that I was not reaching the people who may need my support and encouragement. So, I decided that I am doing things my own way. Those perfect feeds? Good for them! If it brings those people joy, then I say keep at it. If it is a façade, and stressful for you, I say take some time to think about your purpose on Instagram, or any social media.

As a life and wellness coach, my goal on social media is to inspire, entertain, teach, and encourage others. How is putting fake pictures going to serve my audience? It is not! So, instead, I post about gluing my coffee mug into our gingerbread house (no joke!). I show people that I am real, and that there is no need for perfection. It does not serve me or others well.

I breathe
and
I let go.

CHAPTER FOUR

THE DANGER OF PERFECTION

If you have been feeling fatigued, depressed, anxious or physically ill, it may be a sign that the stress of trying to live a perfect existence is creating havoc within your body. When your body is in a state of stress all of the time from trying to have this perfect façade of a life, it can really affect your health and wellness.

When we are trying to achieve perfection in our lives, we are putting our bodies under a lot of stress. Everything is affected, our anatomy, our biochemistry, and the energetics of our bodies are all affected by our emotions. It is a cycle, so if our emotions are continuously out of balance, it can throw off our anatomy or the biochemistry of our bodies.

Stress is a normal thing, and we all experience stress from time to time. Our bodies are built to have a response to stress that is called a "fight or flight" response. To understand this I want you to picture a bear coming down the street towards you. You start to feel stressed, trying to figure out what to do. Do you stay and fight the bear, or do you run for your life? It is normal to be stressed in this moment. But we as humans are not designed to be in this state of stress for extended periods of time, in fact, 90% of the time, our body should be in a state of rest.

If your body is constantly in a state of fight or flight, a hormone called cortisol is released within your body, which, when in excess, can cause a lot of problems including a suppressed immune system, anxiety, depression, headaches, migraines, digestive issues and more.

Reference: HTTPS://WWW.MAYOCLINIC.ORG/HEALTHY-LIFESTYLE/STRESS-MANAGEMENT/IN-DEPTH/STRESS/ART-20046037.

This is what happened to me in my student teaching experience. The level of stress I was experiencing was so high, that it started creating health issues that were debilitating for me.

This experience was the start of my symptoms of autoimmune disease. Autoimmune disease can show up in so many ways in our body. It can be diseases like lupus, and multiple sclerosis, and it can also be joint pain, muscle pain, migraines, food sensitivities, allergies, and skin diseases like hives. The list goes on and on. Over time it can damage and put stress on your organs like your kidneys, liver, and your brain.

So, let's do a little health check. Take a few moments here and ask yourself some questions:

- Are you tired all the time?
- Have you gained weight?
- Are you inflamed, in pain, have headaches or digestive issues?
- Are you sad, angry, or anxious?
- Do you sleep well at night?

It is important to understand that stress may be causing the symptoms that you are experiencing, and once you understand that you can make a plan to start moving forward, and to start feeling better.

Learning to Let Go of Perfection

Now that the light bulb has "switched on" for you, and you have gained an awareness, and maybe you have made some connections, it is time to start learning to let go of perfection.

The first step that helped me was to work on forgiveness. Whether it is forgiving others who may have pressured you to be perfect, willingly or unwillingly, and also to forgive yourself for the pressures and unrealistic expectations that you have put upon yourself, that may have hurt you and/or the ones that you love. We need to let go of the guilt that we have from past mistakes. If we don't, and we continue to hold onto that guilt, of feeling bad about what we've done or what we've missed out on, that can lead to things like depression, anger and frustration.

The next step is to create a list of daily practices that will help keep you present and centered. It is going to take practice to start letting go of perfection because it is so ingrained into everything you do. It is kind of like a favorite coat; your perfectionism is sometimes a coping mechanism for when things do get stressful. If you can create an illusion of perfection and put on a happy façade, then at least everything on the outside looks better. I have created a daily routine of seven practices I do every day to help me stay present. These practices help me to stay focused on being in the present moment.

When you let go, you will feel so free. When I was a little girl, I loved to act out plays. Acting helped me escape to someplace different and fun. Sometimes life can seem like one big play, but when you let go of expectations of perfectionism, you don't have to act anymore; you can just be present and happily YOU. You can enjoy the things that are happening now. You can let others help you. You can let go of having to do everything yourself. You will have more time to do the things you like to do, instead of the things you thought you had to do.

You will be able to enjoy your family and your children, being present with them in the moment, instead of worrying about if your floors are clean, or the cookies are baked. Kids want to play a game or go for a bike ride, but it is dinner time? Go ahead, it is okay if you eat take-out for a night. Have a chance for a beach day, or sledding with friends? Guess what? It is okay to let the laundry wait until tomorrow. Really, unless you have no clean underwear, what will it hurt, waiting one more day?

You are not only letting go of this need for perfection for yourself, but you are also letting go of this for your family and children. You are creating a new pattern of behavior for your children, so that they do not become a victim to a need for perfection, like you were.

You are breaking the chains of perfection!

Good enough is
really good
enough.

CHAPTER FIVE

PERFECTION AND SUCCESS

Perfectionists and work are an uneasy pair! Perfectionists at work are many times smart and very detail oriented. But on the other hand, they can spend hours upon hours trying to get a project just right. They have trouble delegating, for fear that someone else will not be able to do as well on the project as they would. They are often critical of themselves, and others. Some will miss deadlines because they are not able to get the project done exactly as they had pictured them in their mind.

So, how about you? Take a few moments here and ask yourself some questions:

- Are you a perfectionist at work?
- Has it affected relationships with your co-workers?
- Do you miss deadlines, trying to perfect a presentation?
- Do you delegate to others, or do you work long hours doing everything yourself?
- Are you truly happy at your job?
- Are you fulfilling your purpose? Are you doing meaningful work?
- Who is putting that pressure on you to be perfect? Is it your boss? Or is it you?

Trying to do everything perfectly at work sent me down a spiral of illness for years. When you are a perfectionist at work, what is the cost to your family? What is the cost to your health? What is the cost of time with your friends? You've got to have balance in your world. What cost is that perfection to you?

For some people the currency of success is the most important thing, what other currencies are important to you? What about the currency of relationships, the currency of connection, the currency of inner peace, or the currency of legacy?

If a person is constantly seeking perfection, they probably don't have a fulfilling life. They are constantly focused on doing a perfect job, having a perfect family, having perfect Christmas card photos, and having the perfect house. By doing these things they are literally working themselves to death, and not actually enjoying the beautiful life that they already have. Life is passing them by each day.

When I was constantly striving for perfection, trying to do everything myself, it was completely debilitating and depressing for me. I think back to this time in my life, when I was 30 years old and I could barely get out of bed, and it makes me sad. I was constantly in pain, and I truly didn't understand why I was so sick until years later. I honestly would never have admitted that the stress was making me sick back then- that would have been a sign of weakness to me. I wanted to be the best and do the best at work. I also wanted to be able to enjoy my life and have fun. I just didn't know how to get better and make that happen. I didn't know how to balance work and family and do everything well.

At that time, I was newly married, and I couldn't wait to start a family, and to travel. I wanted to be able to enjoy my job because I loved working with children, and they brought me so much joy- but I wasn't enjoying anything. I was sick, tired and depressed. It was a very difficult time, and I could barely function to do the things I needed to do.

My quality of life was suffering. I remember something as simple as going with my husband to his family's house, which was an hour away, and I would count the hours to leave so I could go back home to bed. Not that I didn't want to be there-I was just so exhausted I could not function. I could go to work, do my job, but then everything else would suffer. I was living in a fog of exhaustion and despair.

I am showing up and that is everything!

CHAPTER SIX

WHEN YOU ARE SURVIVING, BUT NOT THRIVING

I see a lot of clients whose bodies are out of balance with many different symptoms. I see women who have gained weight and they don't feel good about themselves. I see women who are in constant pain in their joints and muscles and have a body full of inflammation. My heart hurts seeing other women who are not able to live the life they want because their health is so negatively affected by stress.

That is where I was. I was surviving, but I was not thriving. I have a motto that I try to live by now and remind myself of everyday. We are given this one chance to live our lives. Each day that goes by, and we are sick and in bed, or stressed and angry- we don't get those days back. They are wasted as we are in survival mode.

I don't want you to look back and have regrets for those days lost- the past is in the past. I work with women to help them feel better now, so that each day in the future they can live out their dreams and their purpose. If we don't make the changes, the result is to continue day after day, month after month, year after year, feeling tired, sick, depressed, and not enjoying life. There is no progress or joy, just sadness and regret.

I am more than enough
and I am exactly
where I need to be
right now.

SECTION 2

LIGHTBULB MOMENTS

CHAPTER SEVEN

LIGHTBULB MOMENTS

I have had these little lightbulb moments that came through in my life, and the more that I have learned about health, wellness and balance, the brighter those moments shone back on my past. I have been able to relate all of my bouts of illness and anxiety to stressful times in my life.

Back when I was student teaching, I was very sick, and then when I was teaching full time again a few years ago, it happened again. This second episode of illness was one of the hardest, if not the most difficult times in my life.

It was my rock bottom, and it was the final lightbulb moment that changed my life forever.

A few years ago, I lost my mom. My mom had been sick for several years, and she was in the late stages of Alzheimer's disease. At that time, I was working full-time teaching Kindergarten. It was my first time working full time since having my son, who was in middle school. It was like a perfect storm of stressful things happened all at once. I was already stressed and was getting sick often. My mom passed away right after Thanksgiving, and I was out of work for week.

I returned to work, not quite ready, but I needed to get back for the children. My job was very stressful, and it was a difficult week that week. On the Monday I returned to work; my son was texting me about how awful his day had been. At the time my son was being bullied through social media, and we were trying to work with his school to get it resolved. When a child is being bullied, it affects the whole family, and I was constantly anxious and stressed over it. This particular day was really bad, and he was on the bus, on his way home to an empty house, and he texted me about how down he was feeling.

My anxiety was through the roof, I couldn't go home after being out of work for a week, and as I sat at a staff meeting, my son kept texting me. I could not breathe. I am so thankful for my partner teacher Dayna who helped me through that meeting and through the whole week as I broke down in tears several times. The next day, I was at work and got a call from my allergist, who told me that I had pneumonia- no wonder I felt so lousy!! I was seriously falling apart and everything around me was as well. I wasn't doing anything well, I was so sad, and nothing I did was even close to "perfect", as I tried to manage everything that was coming down around me.

I wasn't being the perfect teacher, the perfect wife, the perfect mom, or the perfect daughter. I was being pulled in so many different directions, with huge stressors in every direction. This was my moment- the moment that I finally, shaking, asked for help. It was one of the first times in my life that I said I needed help, and that I let others in to help me. I didn't care anymore if anyone thought I was a failure, or that I was letting them down. I was past that point and knew things needed to change. I needed to heal.

That was my turning point. I realized that I couldn't do everything on my own. The lightbulb came on, really, really brightly this time.

Stress created a storm in my body of sickness, fatigue, anxiety, and sadness. Sometimes, as women, we experience a lot of stress, and that may show up as physical illness, or fatigue, and then we don't know why we are feeling this way, why we have aches and pains, why are hormones are out of whack, or why our hair is literally falling out of our heads. When I help women to take a really close look at their lives, at their patterns and their values, and what is happening in their lives, they start to put those things together.

The puzzle pieces start to fit together, and the lightbulb starts to shine. These women are able to really see through a new, clear lens, the stress that they are under, either that they create themselves, or is just from trying to balance everything in life, and they start to understand how the stress is really affecting their health and wellness.

So many people deal with the symptoms of their illness, like the headaches, or the sleeplessness, or low mood, but they are not looking at the bigger picture. They may put a quick band-aid on it: taking a sleeping pill, or trying a special diet, but they are not putting the pieces together. It is not just about the symptoms; those are actually the clues that something bigger is going on. It is really about diving in and figuring out what is causing this stuff to happen to your body in the first place.

That lightbulb coming on can be enlightening, frightening, or exciting. For me it was a sense of relief. I now knew why these things were happening- why I was at times sad, anxious, overwhelmed, frustrated, angry and sick. I was at a point where I could let it go. It was like a movie reel went off in my mind of all the times I strived for perfection; wanting things to be a certain way, trying to be everything to everyone- trying to create this sense of perfection, instead of being real, and letting others in to help.

It was so freeing!!! I started to think, who cares if I can't do everything perfectly? I forgave myself for not being able to do it all, and I gave myself permission to start to heal. I learned the importance that giving my best effort is enough. That I may not always be able to be everything to everyone. I learned that giving my best was good enough, and that my best can be different than being perfect.

CHAPTER EIGHT

LETTING GO

When you are a Type A personality or perfectionist, letting go of control is really hard, because now you don't know what is coming. I tried to control everything. This happened even in our home- especially when I was first married. I didn't like the way my husband folded the towels, so I did that. I didn't like the way he folded my shirts, so I would do that too. I didn't like what he bought at the grocery store, so I did the shopping. I needed to have control. It was just easier for me to do it all myself, because then it would be done "the right way", which was my way.

Why did I do things like this? What happened was that I was controlling what I could control in the world, because the world is chaotic. Has this happened to you? You're trying to put these little pieces of control in place. Then you start trying to control everything, you do everything yourself, because it is "easier" and you think no one can do it as well as you can. You then at some point reach a breaking point, where you realize you can't do this anymore. You're not letting anyone in to help you, and the result is stress, anxiety, sickness, and all the things I experienced.

Perfectionists try to control that which is fundamentally uncontrollable. The world is going to do what it is going to do. Nature is going to do what it is going to do. You can't control it.

CHAPTER NINE

EXAMINING YOUR VALUE SYSTEM

After my "lightbulb" moment, I started meditating and practicing mindfulness. I did a lot of reflecting and examining my habits and values. I looked back at where the perfectionism came from. Why did I feel this way? I think it had a lot to do with my parents, though unintentional on their part.

My mom always wanted our home to look perfect. My dad was in the army and then was a police officer, so everything he always did was so neat and organized. I loved when he would tuck me in at night because he made a bed with hospital corners- I seriously could not move when he tucked me into those covers. I grew up with this story of perfection. Maybe in other people's eyes it was different, but this is what I believed to be true.

When I was eighteen years old, my parents separated. As any child of divorce will tell you this is an extremely devastating thing to go through. Your world, no matter how old you are, is turned completely upside down, and will never be the same again. I had no idea up until right before they separated that anything was wrong, because my mom and dad always put on this image that we were the perfect family, and that everything was fine. It was completely gut-wrenching sadness for me. My parents never fought in front of us, which was a lesson learned for me and my own marriage. My husband and I are best friends, but even friends disagree sometimes. And when we disagree, I feel that it is okay for my son to hear and know that. I don't want him growing up and thinking our marriage is a Disney fairy tale. Although we are very happy, we are human! It takes work and lots of love and patience and sometimes a disagreement or two. But to me, that is a healthy way to present a relationship.

When I was pregnant with my son, my mom, who had been a stay-at-home mom too, kept telling me that I was the perfect baby. I slept all the time. I slept while they played cards, and I was in the playpen and was just "the perfect baby." I remember when my son was six days overdue, and there was this weekend that I was back and forth to the hospital. Labor would start and stop. I was in tears with sharp pains of back labor, and I called my friend. I remember saying to her, "It is not supposed to be like this"! I had a perfect, all-natural birth planned. I ended up with an epidural and Pitocin to get the labor going. I pushed to deliver my son for three and a half hours. And then my son cried from the moment he was born. He cried probably for the first three months. He was colicky, he was fussy, and had food allergies we didn't know about, but I thought I was doing something wrong, because everything was going wrong, and I had thought it would be perfect. And he was perfect- a tiny, beautiful human being, who was imperfectly perfect.

My mom had kept saying that I was perfect, so I had this silly notion that my child was going to be perfect. I really thought something was wrong with me and became very anxious as a new mom because of those pressures. I believe I had post-partum depression but didn't even know or understand that at the time. I was so disappointed in my abilities as a mom. My stress was making my son stressed, and it was a constant struggle for me. I wish I could go back and have a redo, but that is not possible. Instead, I forgive myself for my past mistakes, and I work now to be the most chill mom I know how to be to the amazing son that I have!

Now it is time again for you to reflect. To me, happiness is a great indicator of how perfectionism is affecting your life. I recommend you sit and think about whether you are truly happy.

How happy are you on a scale of one to ten? If you are a low number, why is that number low? What is it that is making you unhappy?

How happy are you in these areas of your life?

- Family
- Friends
- Community
- Work

When I was winning the perfection game, I loved it when my parents were proud of me. It made me happy to make them happy. Then that became a pattern of making other people happy with my achievements. I was looking for approval from my mom, my dad, and my husband.

I felt it internally as well, but I was also looking outward for that award or trophy, but what I really wanted was their praise and the knowledge that they thought highly of me. Then I worked hard to flip the switch, to do things that make me happy, instead of looking for that outside, or extrinsic motivation. Really that needs to come from within, and not from pleasing others. It needs to intrinsically motivate from within, rather than extrinsically, or from the outside. I needed to learn that lesson.

I'm imperfect
and I am
still enough.

CHAPTER TEN

AM I REALLY A PERFECTIONIST?

If you are not sure whether you are a perfectionist or not, look at why you are doing things.

Here are a few questions to ask yourself:

- Are you doing things for you, or for appearances to show the picture of perfection to others?
- How healthy and happy are you?
- How fulfilled do you feel?
- Do you feel fulfilled by your life?

I had to examine all of that.

I looked back at different times of my life when I was highly stressed and ended up sick. But what caused the stress? It was me trying to control everything. It was me trying to make everything perfect.

It is like when they do contact tracing with a virus. You want to go right back to the beginning and find patient zero. Where did it start? What is the reason we try to control the uncontrollable?

I am mindful and in the present.

CHAPTER ELEVEN

MINDFULNESS

One of the key practices that has helped me to stay present, and not be anxious, is to practice mindfulness. Being mindful means to be here in the present moment, not worrying about things in the future, or dwelling on the past.

One thing that helps me to practice mindfulness is using a gratitude journal. Every morning when I get up, I think about what I am thankful for. When you practice gratitude, things really do change! There is now a lot of scientific evidence to back this up. People who practice gratitude are actually happier, and for those of us whose stress causes illness, studies have shown that practicing gratitude can actually support your immune system.

If you are trying to let go of perfection and want to practice being more present in your daily life, I recommend having an accountability partner. I'm really lucky mine lives with me; it's my husband. My husband is someone who lives in the present. He is not worried about what happened yesterday, or anyone's opinions of us, or our home. He works hard, he is a great dad and wonderful husband, and he keeps things real in our home. When I would get out of control trying to keep the house perfect, he would help to set me straight.

Did you ever see the movie with Julia Roberts, Sleeping with the Enemy? Her husband was obsessive compulsive and wanted everything perfect. I used to be like that (well the obsessive with the house part!) I lined up remotes on the table, toys were lined up, towels would be hanging neatly and at the same length. After I saw that movie, I realized that I was becoming obsessive like that!

My husband helped me get passed this. When I used to line up all the towels perfectly, he would mess them up.

I would line up all of the remotes, and he would move them. I would get so mad at him. But, then I started laughing at how silly I was being. I gradually got past everything needing to be perfect.

You start coming into your own, becoming comfortable with yourself, and letting your inner self shine through. You let down your guard, that shield of perfection. When you do, it is like a mask comes off, and you can show who you truly are. Your gifts, and your flaws. Your perfectly imperfect self.

I am uniquely and happily me.

CHAPTER TWELVE

UNDERSTANDING YOUR PERSONALITY

Have you ever taken a personality test? One of my favorites is the Color Personality Test by Jacob Adamo. There are four color personalities in this test. Red is a risk taker, a take charge kind of person. Blue wants to have fun! Yellow is caring and helpful, thinking of others, and green is analytical and logical.

For a lot of my life, I was trying to be something I wasn't, so when I did this color personality quiz, it was a real ah-ha moment for me. I came out as red and blue. I have a "go getter" personality, and I am a risk taker, but I also have a side to me that really likes to have fun.

My friends will tell you; I am the first to sign up for a race. Want to go on a trip? My bags are already packed! Then there is my husband, he is the complete opposite of me! My husband tested as a green personality.

This test really helped me because for so long I tried to be more yellow. I really wanted to be the kind and caring one. You know the ones, those amazing people thinking of the birthday gifts two weeks ahead of time, and baking cookies for the neighbor who just had a baby, never forgetting a card, or bringing things to people who are sick.

I wanted to be that person, and I really tried to be that perfect mom and friend. I just am not really wired that way. I wanted to be, I tried to be. But I am more of the send a gift card at the last-minute person, because I am doing a million other things, and ideas are always running through my mind.

I do believe my friends will tell you that I'm kind and caring, but I'm more focused on work and other things than being a "Pinterest Mom". When I started to accept who I really was, it was such a relief. What I do have to share with the world is big ideas, leading people, and helping people with their health and wellness through those things.

Stress comes in when you are trying to be a perfect you that is opposite of your core personality. If you are doing what you naturally like to do, it likely gives you little stress and lots of joy. Whether you used color personalities, Myers Briggs Personality Type Indicators, or the DISK Personality style, it is really about accepting who you are, and acknowledging your pathway to perfectionism may tread a different road than someone who is a different personality type.

What a relief!! I finally accepted who I was. A snapshot of the real me: My desk is almost never neat; I have 50 windows open on my computer which drives my husband and son crazy. I am messy. When I am brainstorming and working on projects, I can get lost in that for a long time. I lose track of time and so I end up am throwing dinner together and praying it comes out okay! It's just who I am, and it is so freeing to have these expectations I put on myself gone.

Doing this color personality test also helped me understand and accept my husband and son. My husband is the opposite of me, and my son is a mixture of both of us. My husband is very analytical and logical, so if someone says we are going to do something, he needs all the information to understand and make a decision. And now I understand when my son asks me 50 questions, I need to be patient and answer them.

We humans are all unique and we all bring something different to the table. Trying to be something you are not is only going to cause you stress. You can't control your personality.

There is not only one way to be successful, and there is not only one personality type that can be successful. We need to embrace our style, start exploring what our personality types need, and what success means to us.

I don't sweat the
small stuff.

CHAPTER THIRTEEN

DON'T SWEAT THE SMALL STUFF

Sometimes I have to laugh at myself and at what used to matter to me- the really meaningless things I used to stress over. When we first got married, I got so upset with my husband when the grass wasn't mowed and perfect, and my husband couldn't understand why.

When I was growing up, my father would sit out and water the grass until it was perfect, so I expected our yard to look that way as well. My dad seemed to love to sit on the front step, watering the grass. I didn't understand why my husband was out fishing with his friends when our grass was long, and he should have been cutting it. I used to stress so much about how the yard looked, and if the flowers were trimmed, and the grass was perfect.

Now there are days my husband and I sit by the pool and don't worry whether the grass has been watered or cut, or if there are (gasp!) weeds in the garden. It is so freeing to be able to just enjoy life and enjoy the moments when my husband is off work, my son is home, or we have family around.

My relationships with my son and husband have changed, in that we spend more time together and don't sweat the small stuff. We would rather do something as a family, watch a movie, hang out on the deck, or just talk and be together. That has always been important, but now it's the most important thing and all the other stuff can wait.

The best advice one of my friends Renee told me once was that her house was clean enough. I loved that and it really has made a difference to me. That is how I live now. My house is clean enough, the yard looks good

enough, now let's just enjoy each other and our life together.

I let go of
perfection with
joy and ease.

SECTION 3

THE COST OF PERFECTION

CHAPTER FOURTEEN

THE COST OF PERFECTION

When I hit my "rock bottom" a few years ago, I was at a point where I needed help. I always tried to just get through things on my own, or just push through. This time, I couldn't.

Some things I remember so clearly- they stood out in my mind. Just before the "storm" exploded, I had an argument with my husband. He and I may disagree once in a while, but we rarely have a big argument. I remember he was trying to help with dinner. He was taking over so much for me in the house, because I was so over-whelmed, and he wanted to help me. This particular night, he was making American Chop Suey, and we were arguing because he put too much sauce in it. I was so upset I went in my room and cried for an hour and a half.

My son came in and asked if I was going to be okay, and I couldn't stop crying. I was so upset over something so silly. I didn't know it, but I was depressed. It was one of my first experiences with depression, aside from what I also believe may have been post-partum depression when my son was born. At this time, I wanted to drive away and never come back. I had a fleeting thought of wanting to drive into a tree and for everything to just be over. I was so tired, and I just could not handle the pain and the stress anymore. It became too much to bear.

Even though I loved my family and friends and had all these great things in my life, the stress of everything on my shoulders was too much. When I reached out to my doctor and asked for help, that was a lightbulb moment that it was okay to ask for help. It was such a simple thing, but so hard for me. But, when I asked for help, I actually felt the biggest sense of relief.

When I asked for help, I started my recovery process with not only my physical health, but my mental health as well.

I am going to be super honest, it was really scary for a while, because I felt like it was never going to get better, and that I wasn't strong enough to handle things. I was ashamed and embarrassed that I couldn't handle everything, and that I had let everyone down. My husband. My son. My sister. My job. My students. Their parents. I felt desperate. I thought I wasn't going to get back to the way it was before all of this happened to me.

And then, to my great relief, I started to heal. I learned that through reaching out for help, there is hope. I knew I had a husband who was supportive, my son who was supportive, and my sister who texted me every day with a cheerful photo or words of encouragement to make me feel better. Even though they were there for me, it was when I reached out to my doctor and she suggested I talk to a therapist, that things started to click for me. Talking to someone who was a neutral party helped me so much!

One thing that I want you to know, even in your darkest moments, there is always hope. One of the things I talked about in an earlier chapter is gratitude. Even in those dark days, I practiced that gratitude. I would say I'm thankful for my dog; I'm thankful for my husband; I'm thankful for my son. I am thankful for my sister. Even if that was all I could say, I would say that every single day.

I found that even in my darkest days, even though it seemed like there was no hope, there really is if you reach out. There is someone who can help you.

My best friend Sue used to call me her perfect friend- and I thank her for it, but I was far from it. I was trying to be "Super Mom", doing everything I could to support my son. I was back at work full-time for the first time since he was born. I felt the pressure of wanting to do my job well, trying to be a good wife, and trying to be a good daughter to a mom who was in the last stages of her life. It was daunting to ask for help.

But it was the best thing I have ever done for my physical health and mental health. When you are used to being the strong one, the one people lean on, then all of a sudden you are the one who needs help, it's humbling. It puts a whole different perspective on life and what is important.

At first, I felt ashamed by what happened. I was embarrassed that I had failed. I felt guilty that I chose to heal and not return to my classroom. There is also such a stigma with mental illness. Like if you are depressed or anxious, it is not real, or you are weak. Slowly I started to be brave and share with people that I had broken down. I shared what I had been through, and how everything had gotten to be too much for me. I felt if I could share what happened to me, the woman who looks like she has it together on the outside, maybe it would help someone else. It took a lot of courage to admit that I couldn't handle everything, and that the cape had fallen off this Super Mom.

I learned through this process it is okay to not be perfect, and it is okay to just be me- I don't have to be a Super Mom all alone, in fact it is kind of like my favorite Saturday morning cartoon from when I was little- the *Super Friends*. I have a whole "squad" of people to help me. No one is expecting perfection from me, or for me to do everything alone. This process also taught me to be honest, and not walk in my pain alone. No one is meant to be perfect. Everyone is flawed. I wear those messages on my sleeve now.

Your Mental and Physical Health

My autoimmune disease started back when I was student teaching, when I was under a lot of stress. Throughout the years, every time I have been in a stressful situation, I have had autoimmune flare ups. When I went through the last stressful time period, the stress affected me mentally and physically. One of the most devastating things to happen to me was that I developed an allergy to the cold.

One of my forms of stress relief is running. I love running, and I enjoy it so much with my friends every weekend. One morning, a few weeks before my mom passed away, I was running before school. I started to feel light-headed, and then started to cough. I looked down and noticed I had hives on my legs. I ran home and saw that I was covered from the neck down in the hives. I jumped in the shower. I was able to warm my body up, and started to feel okay again, but I was scared.

I went to my allergist and he told me I have cold-induced anaphylaxis and that I now had to now run with an Epi Pen. I am allergic to the cold, living in New England! Not fun!! Not being able to run in the cold was devastating to me, because that was my stress relief. I no longer could join my friends, and I became panicky when the temperature would drop below 50 degrees.

Autoimmune diseases present in different ways for different people. It is the body's immune system turning on itself and acting in a counter intuitive way. For many of us, it lies dormant while we are mentally healthy and not stressed, and our bodies can keep it in check. But as soon as the body loads with stress, these dormant things awaken and have profound effects on our lives.

Once I realized stress was a cause of these illnesses; the headaches, the hives and so on, it was a great relief. Now, at least, I know my mental and physical health have to be my number one priority. I want to be around to enjoy life and live out my purpose, but I can't do that if I am not healthy.

The Dangers to Your Health

Is the stress of perfectionism affecting your health?

One of the first signs of health issues is fatigue. If you are tired all the time, you may want to stop and evaluate your health.

Here are a few questions:

- On a scale of 1-10, how do you feel most days?
- What is your energy like?
- How do you sleep?
- Do you exercise?
- Are you feeling peaceful and calm every day?
- Or are you angry and frustrated? Or are you sad?

When you are angry, that can affect your physical health, as well as your energy. If you are sad, that affects your energy.

Think about these questions:

- Have you gained weight?
- Do you feel inflamed?
- Are you in pain?
- Do you have brain fog?
- Do you have sinus headaches or migraines?

That can all be related to stress- when we strive for perfection, as we have talked about- it can really wreak havoc on your physical and mental health.

Asking for Help

There is no shame in asking for help when it comes to your mental health. Your mental health is just as important as your physical health. Your mental health affects your physical health. There are so many resources that I will share with you that can help.

The stigma of showing you need help with your mental health, or that you are not a whole person, is not true. The stressors between family, work, finances and so on, can bring on anxiety and depression, which can affect your physical health as well.

I will never forget the time that a doctor told me that it was all in my head, that my autoimmune disease was depression or some kind of excuse. He made me feel like I was a "weak" woman, and that I was making things up. I am telling you; it is real! Stress can cause both mental and physical health issues. It is not all in your head, because what is going on in your head impacts or can be impacted your body as well. Thankfully today, mental health is being understood on a deeper level.

> *Maintaining mental health is an important part of every person's life.*

A lot of people don't talk about depression or anxiety, so we don't know our friend, or neighbor, or co-workers are also suffering. Sometimes for example, with a migraine, you can take medication and go into a dark room, and that's the quickest solution to feel better. Mental health can take longer to recover from. For someone like me who was a perfectionist, my mind was always going, I was constantly worrying, and constantly having stress in my body. It was really difficult to let go of, and it took time to learn how to manage it with the right tools. It was not something anyone could see on the outside, but it was something that affected me deeply on the inside.

Anxiety and Perfectionism

Anxiety is this feeling that comes up over you. It can feel like somebody's squeezing your chest, or maybe your heart is racing out of control. It can come up out of the blue or be situational. For me it was mostly situational.

When I was stressed in my job, I felt it. I couldn't breathe. When my son was going home on the bus to an empty house feeling upset about being bullied, my heart was racing, and my throat felt like it was closing. In therapy, I learned to practice mindfulness, which really helped with anxiety. My therapist taught me that when we are in the present, we are mindful, but when we are anxious, we are worrying about things in the future, things that we cannot control.

Depression and Perfectionism

I also learned about depression, and when we start fixating on things in the past, that can lead to feelings of guilt and depression. I felt so guilty about not being good at everything I was managing- family, home and work. As I dwelled on it, and my current situation, I was becoming depressed. Practicing mindfulness helped me with this.

It is helpful to examine the things that cause you stress from your life and to see if you can eliminate them one by one. It is okay to stop doing things that cause you undue stress. I left my job to heal – it was causing me a lot of stress, and by leaving I could heal mentally and physically. It also allowed me to be more present as a wife and mom. Being present for my family, along with my health, was the most important thing to me.

My health is more
important than my
accomplishments

CHAPTER FIFTEEN

CREATE HEALTHIER HABITS

It is important to create a toolbox of practices to support your mental health. It can be anything from diet and exercise, to mindfulness and meditation. It helps to have some go-to tools that you can put into place that work for you in your situation, when you feel you are suffering from anxiety or depression.

If at any time you feel unsafe, it is very important to get in touch with a healthcare provider.

When you are in a state of anxiety or depression and need to access mindfulness, sometimes taking note of your physical surroundings can help, it is something that has helped me. There is a corner of the room, there is a window, there is a chair, the chair is cold, I can feel myself breathing, and so on. These things can help you get out of worrying about the past or concerning yourself about the future and bring you into the present moment.

Creating Boundaries

Take a close look at the relationships in your life that are supportive, as well as those that are toxic. When I was going through my "rock bottom" ordeal, there were people putting too much pressure on me, which was affecting my health and wellness, and I had to create boundaries to protect myself. They weren't always liked, but I needed to protect myself during the healing process.

It is okay to take care of your own health and wellness, and not be the person everyone calls, or needs all the time. You don't have to answer every text or phone call right away. We have become a society where everything is expected to happen NOW. If you don't answer a text right away, the person sending it thinks something is wrong! You have the right to take time for yourself. I had to put up boundaries during that time so I could take care of me. I couldn't take care of everyone else at that time. If someone else cannot handle it, that is on them, not you. If they can't respect your need to heal, then you may want to rethink that person's place in your life.

For perfectionists, creating boundaries can be incredibly difficult. We are not good at telling people "no" or saying, "I don't want to do that." It offends our sense of perfectionism. I have learned the art of saying "no" to things I don't want to do, so I can say "yes" to things that bring me joy. And the best part, I am letting go of the guilt that I may be letting others down with my "no".

I used to say "yes" all the time, trying to make everyone happy, then what would happen was that I would be taking on too much, or something I didn't want to do. Now, I only help when I truly can and want to. Instead of offering to do things either I am not good at, or something that is too time consuming for me, I find other ways to help. Learning to say "no" has been huge for me, because when I take on things I don't really want to do, or have the time to do, it creates stress for me. Then I become frustrated with myself for spreading myself too thin.

Typical Stressors for Perfectionists

For many perfectionists, we get stressed about outward appearances. One of those is how our home looks to others. When I was a stay-at-home mom, I felt that my house had to be in perfect, tip-top shape. I washed the floors so often that you "could eat off them", I baked everything from scratch, and my house was perfectly decorated. I looked for those outer, extrinsic rewards or praise from others thinking I did a good job.

I was so hung up on having a house that was perfect that I actually had a schedule! I had a weekly and monthly cleaning schedule. The idea of that is not really a bad thing- it just made me stressed when we didn't get it all done. Every January, I went through every single closet and organized them. In February, I would go around and touch up paint. In March, I would spring clean. I had a binder to make sure everything was in order and looked great. Again, it is actually wonderful to be organized, but not if that "to do" list is not done, and that stresses you out!

When I was growing up, Christmas was a big deal. We had a finished, paneled basement, and every Thanksgiving weekend we had to wash the paneling with Murphy's Oil soap, the smell of it still reminds me of Christmas. We cleaned the basement from top to bottom, before any decorating took place. When our family decorated the tree, our ornaments had to be "just so". My mom would get on a ladder and measure how she put up the garland. I really don't think my mom was doing that to stress us out, I think she thought it was a reflection on her how everything looked, and she took pride in everything looking perfect.

When I grew up, got married and had my own house, I took that on. When we first had our home, I went completely overboard at Christmas. My house was decorated with candles in every window, garlands on the fence, lights everywhere, and bows on the chairs. I cooked seven course meals no one wanted to eat. I thought that's what it looked like to have the perfect Christmas.

Then, as the lightbulb started switching on for me, and I was re-evaluating my life, I realized all of a sudden, I didn't really like decorating for Christmas, and I didn't even want Christmas to come. It wasn't fun. It was so much work. I was exhausted trying to make everything look perfect and I wasn't enjoying it. I also realized that I didn't want to pass that on to my son, so I needed to make sure I made things fun and easy. We got rid of a lot of the stuff that didn't please anybody in our home. I learned that it was not about pleasing anyone else, or looking for that extrinsic reward of praise, and that's when we started doing things that were fun.

Want to know a question I ask clients that helps me get a feel for if they may be a perfectionist? I ask them whether they move the decorations around on their Christmas tree after their kids put them on. If they do, it is a sign they may have a bit of work to do. I admit, I used to do it too, but for years now, I leave everything the way it is, and I truly love it that way.

The Art of Saying "No"

It is hard to say "no" because you want to be there for everyone. But then you run yourself ragged and spread yourself too thin, that is when the stress builds up which can affect your mental and physical health.

It is also about learning to say "yes" to the things that bring you joy, that are fun, or are meaningful to you and your family. Sometimes we have to say "yes" because it is the right thing to do, someone needs our help, or it is something for our children.

We have the choice to think about it and ask:

- Is it worth my time?
- Is this worth my time away from my family?
- Is this worth my time with my family?
- Is this something that is going to bring us joy?

If it is not, then we need to learn to say "no." The more you do it, the easier it gets. It is just fine if people are looking for help and you find a way you can help that maybe works better for you. Maybe it is donating gift cards when people are crafting things for holidays for school or donating books and shipping them from

Amazon. Do what works for you, so you feel like you are contributing, but it is not putting stress on your own life.

I read about this guy who wrote down the names of all of the people who were important in his life on a post-it note. He keeps it in his pocket to remind him they are the people he is willing to be stressed for. These are the people he will go out of his way for. I think it is a great reminder.

When I stressed about the house being perfectly clean, I made a choice. Did it matter if my son remembered me cleaning the house all the time like I remember my mom? Or is it important to remember I went on a bike ride, or we watched a movie, or went to the zoo? That is what I chose.

My friend Renee once said to me her house was clean enough. She probably has no idea how freeing that was for me when I heard that. That is how I live my life now. My house is clean enough, and what is really more important is spending time with my husband and son.

Letting People In

It is okay to ask for help from your family. It is okay to ask for help from your co-workers. As a perfectionist, you are probably used to doing everything and not delegating very much. But if you want to let go and embrace the mess, sometimes that means letting people in and letting them help you.

From the time my son was two, I made banana chocolate chip muffins every week, and my husband and son loved them. When I was working full time, I got to a point where I didn't have time to make them and it was devastating because I was used to being that mom, the mom who baked cookies and muffins. I honestly love doing that for my family, and baking is relaxing for me. But baking was becoming one more chore that put pressure on me.

My husband saw me struggling, trying to do it all, and he said he would make them, and asked me if I could teach him how. It was just one of the gifts he has given me, helping to take something off of my plate, literally! I taught him and, honestly that was such a hard thing for me to let go of. But it gets so much easier. Three years later he's still making them every week, and I don't have to worry about it.

It can be hard at first to give up control of being the one who does everything, or thinking you have to do everything, but it ends up being such a gift in so many ways. When we as a family each do our share, we are able to enjoy more quality time together. My husband is always there to lend a helping hand, which means so much to me, I don't feel that I needed to do everything.

As you start to let go, you realize that "done" is better than perfect. My son has done his laundry since he was ten years old. I taught him how to do it. Is it done perfectly? Nope. Is his closet perfect? No. Do I care? No. The laundry is done, and it is put away. My husband folds the clothes differently than I do, and I used to refold everything! What a waste of time that I can't get back. Now I truly am just happy it is done!

Letting go and letting people who love you and want to help you make your life easier and more enjoyable, is the best thing you can do for yourself. You are all a family together- a unit with different moving pieces. There is no one saying mom has to do everything; mom has to do the carpool; mom has to fill out the school forms; mom has to cook and clean. How is one person expected to work full time, and do everything in the house, and with the kids? Spouses can help and so can your kids. Everyone has to help. Everyone is important. Everyone should be equal. That took me a long time to learn, but once I did, it made life a lot easier.

Time for Forgiveness

When we look at our past patterns and values, many of those have come from our childhood experiences, and from our relationships with our parents, teachers, coaches, and siblings. In order to move forward, and to let go, we must start the process of forgiveness. Forgiveness is generally defined as "a conscious, deliberate decision to release feelings of resentment or vengeance toward a person or group who has harmed you, regardless of whether they actually deserve your forgiveness." (https://greatergood.berkeley.edu/topic/forgiveness/definition)

It may not always be easy to forgive- but, when we forgive others, we can start to move forward, to release the pain, and start to heal. We can start with forgiving our parents. My mom was a perfectionist, and I understand what she was trying to do. Being a stay-at-home mom was her job, and she tried to make a beautiful home and family for me, my sisters, and my Dad.

I know my parents loved me and did the best they could for me. I know they weren't trying to upset me send me into 50 years of striving for perfection. I forgive them because I truly feel they were trying to do what was best for me.

It is a win-win when you forgive. When you hold onto sadness, anger, or frustration, that can really affect your mental and physical health. When you forgive someone, it can be freeing for you and can help create peace within you.

The next person you need to forgive is yourself. As a perfectionist, you have gone through life trying to do everything well. Sometimes you got in your own way trying to get things done or complete projects, and maybe haven't completed the things you wanted to. Maybe you feel guilty because you put stress on yourself to do everything well, and now you're suffering with emotional and physical health issues.

You are seeing the way you lived your life put stress on you, and it doesn't just affect you, but it also affects your family and your co-workers. You need to forgive yourself because you didn't know.

You don't know, until you know. Now that you know, you can make changes. You can start to make connections between your behavior, attitude, health and your past. You make those connections, forgive yourself from past mistakes, let that go, and live for the present. The past is the past, just move on, and try to control the perfection going forward.

When I forgave myself, I felt incredibly free. I didn't feel as much pressure on myself, or that weight of the world on my shoulders all the time. I feel this sense of calm, peace, happiness, and joy. I feel more present, and I enjoy everything that is happening right now. Before I was so worried about how things looked, or getting all the things done, that I spread myself so thin trying to do everything. I wasn't really enjoying the moments, even though I thought I was.

I now realize all the things that were getting in the way of that. By forgiving myself and acknowledging all this, it helped me to be a better wife and mother. I am setting a better example for my son of what is truly important.

SECTION 4

EMBRACING THE MESS AND FINDING YOUR BALANCE

I am exactly where
I am supposed
to be.

CHAPTER SIXTEEN

SHERI'S SEVEN SURVIVAL TIPS FOR LETTING GO AND FINDING YOUR BALANCE

Now it is time to start embracing the mess, accepting life's chaotic moments and reviewing practical steps to help you recover from perfection. The following are called "practices" because they are not something you can just do and check off the list. You have to work on them each day and you're not going to get it perfect right away. On day two you will be better, and day three even better. These practices can help free you up from the perfectionism holding you back.

1. Start Your Day the Right Way
The Power of Affirmations, Meditation and Gratitude

Mindfulness

Mindfulness was explained to me so well by my therapist. He explained to me that when we focus on the past, it can be associated with feelings of guilt, which can lead to depression. When we are constantly worrying about the future, it can create feelings of anxiety.

For me, as a recovering perfectionist, I find that staying in the present helps to keep me on track- and helps me to not worry or to feel guilty. I find that when I focus on today, this hour, this minute, I am able to stay calm, clear, and focused.

I have a morning routine for mindfulness, and all three of these practices can help you stay in the present moment. That is what we are trying to achieve so we can ward off anxiety and depression.

Practicing Gratitude

I have practiced gratitude I saw it on the Oprah Winfrey Show sometime in the late 1990s. I watched her and loved when she shared her gratitude journal. I started writing the three things I was grateful for every day. I still do it today. I usually write down the three things I am grateful for as soon as I wake up. If I can't think of something right then, then I think about something that happened the day before I am grateful for.

Sometimes you are going through a difficult time and you have to dig deep for that gratitude. It might be my husband, my son, my dog, or reading a book in bed, and so on. Whatever it is, gratitude can really help with stress levels and immune health.

It helps you to be thankful more for people and experiences, rather than things. Sometimes as perfectionists we can go towards materialistic things like nice cars, or a nice home, whereas gratitude makes it more personal. Who is in your life, and what things are happening that you are grateful for?

"I am thankful for my husband. Thank you. I'm thankful for my home. Thank you."

I have witnessed this with children as well. When I was an early childhood teacher, every Friday we would have a Gratitude Circle, even with children as young as age three. When we would start our Gratitude Circles at the beginning of the year, the children were grateful for their doll, train, lunchbox, or video game. As time went on, no fail every year, they were grateful for their friend who helped them, their teacher, their mom or dad. It was a beautiful transformation to witness.

Scientists have discovered the act of gratitude, or focusing your mind on what you appreciate, actually has a chemical reaction in your brain. It is almost exactly the same as taking an anti-depression drug like Prozac. The act of saying three things you are grateful for has the same effect as chemical medication. It is an inexpensive and effective tool. It is not fluffy; it is backed by science. There are studies showing it helps relieve stress, pain, depression, and can even boost your immune system.

Affirmations

Affirmations help us to challenge and defeat self-sabotaging thoughts. What you speak to yourself matters. Whether you talk to yourself in a positive way or a negative way, your brain can't tell the difference. When you speak truth and love of yourself, your body and your brain start to believe it as well.

One thing I teach my clients is that if their self- talk is negative, chances are that their outcomes are going to be negative as well. One of the things I say when I coach people is, "If you say you can't, you won't. If you say you can, you will."

Positive thinking and affirmations can help to rewire your brain. If you have been saying to yourself for a year, "I am not good enough" or "Nothing I do is ever enough," you have some work to do.

Affirmations are "I" statements and don't contain negative words, only positive ones. I suggest studying a list of affirmations that are meaningful to you. Say them. Pick one per day and put it on your screensaver on your phone. Tape it on your mirror in your bathroom. Speak that truth over yourself.

I have shared many affirmations with you throughout this book at the beginning of each chapter. Here are a few more to practice:

> *I am enough.*
>
> *I am worthy of just being me.*
>
> *I am strong and confident.*
>
> *I am valued and I am loved.*

Here is a little experiment that you can try. I recommend that you take notice of your self-talk. What are the things you say to yourself all the time? Now imagine that voice in your head turns into someone that sits beside you. Now imagine that person sits beside you and tells you all those things you tell yourself.

Is that someone you want to spend time with? Most people would answer that person is fairly negative and harasses them when they are not perfect. Most people wouldn't want to spend time with a person like that, but that is what you are living with every day.

Think you will forget to say those affirmations? Here is another fun and easy tip! This was shared with me-try putting a little colored dot sticker on your phone or in your car as a reminder to say that affirmation to yourself. Affirmations can really change the way we think and help with that depression and anxiety.

Our brains were built to protect us, but sometimes they don't help when it comes to mental health. Affirmation statements are all about giving an alternative perspective to that negative voice and making the voice in your head someone you want to spend time with.

Prayer

Prayer looks like different things to different people. For the last 10 years or so, I have found great comfort in spending time in prayer each morning. Reading, writing, reflecting, singing, watching, whatever it is for you. Prayer can bring us comfort, and also is a reminder to stay present, to not judge, and to not worry. One of my favorite books to read each morning is *Jesus Calling*, by Sarah Young.

Meditation

Meditation is hard for perfectionists because it is not a perfect science. It is imperfect. It takes time to practice and get used to, and a lot of times we have thoughts in our head, so we feel like we fail.

Once when I was in yoga class, my instructor told us to think of the thoughts coming through our head as clouds floating through. They will come in and out, you can't control them, so let them come and let them go. We shouldn't be angry or frustrated about them. The more you meditate, the better you get at it.

It can start with as little as five minutes a day a couple of times a week and move on from there. I find it helpful whether meditating sitting quietly, or listening to a guided meditation, to say one word over and over to help stay in the moment. I sometimes say "peace" or "joy" as I practice.

Morning Stretch

Some mornings I also take 10-15 minutes to do a light stretch. I grab my yoga mat, some water to sip on, some relaxing music and my essential oils. I do an inhalation of the oils, and then I stretch from head to toe, also sometimes adding in foam rolling. Sometimes, I do this at night, before bed. It helps me to create a peaceful space in my heart as I start the day or helps me to have a good night's sleep. Either way, I get my stretching in every single day.

ACTION PLAN:

Practice Mindfulness:

- Gratitude
- Meditation or Prayer
- Morning Stretches

Notes:

_____

_____

_____

_____

_____

_____

_____

2. Fuel for Your Brain

Writing

Each morning, I set aside 10 minutes for writing. Free writing is giving yourself a bit of time each day to spend on a 'brain dump.' It is putting all of your thoughts out on paper. It helps me to put a timer on. You may wish to start with just five minutes, then work up to 10 minutes each day, then just write.

Writing for me is freeing. It is something I teach my college students to do. Last year I gave them all little notebooks, and we would spend the first 10 minutes of class journaling. It was something that my students enjoyed and looked forward to.

What do I write about? Sometimes I get my thoughts out on paper about how I'm feeling. Sometimes it is bullet lists. Sometimes I write things I want to do, sometimes how to organize my day, and so on. Whatever it is, it is an opportunity to write down my thoughts and feelings.

Sometimes I don't look at it again, but the process of getting it from my brain to paper, and feeling that pen on the paper, is a really special thing. Many professional writers use free writing to warm up each day. There is a little saying in their world, "No great idea ever came out of a keyboard, it usually comes out of a pen and paper." Try working with a pen and paper for this free writing exercise.

Reading

Reading is so important to learn and expand your knowledge. We always have room for improvement, and you can always find books that resonate with you, that you can read each morning. Sometimes I'll read for 10 minutes and write for 10 minutes because something I read might trigger something I want to write as well.

No matter how old we are, we need to keep learning to keep our brains healthy and active. Scientists discovered that brain plasticity means no matter how old you get, the more you learn, the more you are capable of learning.

Like an Olympic athlete trains so they can use their abilities at the right moment, learning is so incredibly important because the more you learn, the more your brain is capable of solving complex problems. The older you get, the more complex your problems are going to be, so it is training you to handle the things that will come up.

Some people have fixed mindsets where they believe they only have a finite amount of intelligence to work with. Others have a growth mindset of neuroplasticity, where we are always learning and expanding our knowledge. The fixed mindset is the old way of thinking. There really is no limit to your intelligence, what you can learn, or your ability to learn, as long as you have a growth mindset.

In their book titled Mindset: The New Psychology of Success, Dr. Carol Dweck et al[1]., promoted the growth mindset, not just for schools and teenagers, but for CEOs and regular people as well. I highly recommend this incredibly profound book. It is something I have used with all of my students as well, from age 3 to adult students.

---

1 DWECK, C. S. (2006). MINDSET: THE NEW PSYCHOLOGY OF SUCCESS. RANDOM HOUSE.

ACTION PLAN:

Schedule 5- 10 minutes for:

- Reading
- Writing

Notes:

_____

_____

_____

_____

_____

_____

_____

3. Fuel for Your Body

Food can either help or hurt your body. It can create a feeling of calmness, peace, and good energy, or it can create more stress, frustration, and anger. When you eat a plant-based diet, you eat a lot of alkaline foods which create calmness. I strive to eat a plant-based diet as much as I can.

When you eat meat, especially those from conventional farms, a lot of these animals are very stressed. When you eat foods from stressed animals, your body takes on that stress. (Check out the documentary Food, Inc.)

When I switched to an organic, non-GMO, plant-based diet, I noticed a shift in my overall energy and mood. It took some time for me to get there. My suggestion is to start researching and making small changes over time. Don't be a perfectionist and do it all right away, as that can set you up for frustration and failure. Just keep in mind your diet can really affect your stress levels.

Not every diet is right for everyone. A plant-based diet works really well for me, but it is important to find the right balance for you. You know your body best, and if you need help, enlist the support of a health coach or nutritionist. Simple changes, such as cutting sugar, and eating organic can make such a big difference in your energy levels.

Many of my health coaching clients have found success with my 5 Week Jumpstart Health Coaching program. One of my clients, who took my Five Week Jumpstart course started to feel more energetic after just a few weeks. Another client had less brain fog and started running in her fifties! Another client found my program to be helpful while recovering from breast cancer.

Each of them had to do the work but saw results that helped them to live a more balanced life. To me, if your health is out of balance, it is really hard to find balance with work, friends, and family.

ACTION PLAN:

Find a healthy + energizing
diet that works to support
your health

Notes:

_____

_____

_____

_____

_____

_____

_____

_____

4. Rejuvenate with Exercise and Sleep

Exercise

Exercise releases endorphins like serotonin, which is a happy hormone. When you are feeling stressed, one of the best things you can do is to exercise, which will help to create balance in your life.

If you have not exercised before, start off small, it could be a 10 minute walk a few days a week, then you might add things like stretching or yoga, then work towards 30 to 60 minutes a day.

I do Jeff Galloway's "run-walk-run" program which is proven to help release more endorphins. (Check out Jeff's Programs at www.jeffgalloway.com) Running has really helped me with stress. When I had my issues with the cold weather and I couldn't run outside, I made some changes and started using a treadmill inside. It was really important to help manage my stress.

Exercise comes in all forms. I love running, but martial arts is wonderful for creating good energy, as is CrossFit, yoga, strength training, bike riding, hiking, swimming, surfing, whatever works for you. What is important is to move your body.

Sleep

Our bodies need seven to eight hours of sleep a night to maintain, prepare, and repair. As a perfectionist, I would go to sleep, then at 3:00 am I would wake up and my brain would start going. Sleep hygiene, or having a good night-time routine, is important. Things like sleeping in a cool room, having a warm shower before bed, and using essential oils, can signal to your body it is time to sleep.

I have always felt like if I can sleep, I can handle anything. If you can't sleep, problems arise that seem bigger than they really are.

When you allow yourself to be rejuvenated, whether through exercise or sleep, you are much calmer, able to handle what comes to you, able to make good decisions, and prioritize things.

If you are stressed and sleep deprived, it is hard to enjoy all that's in front of you.

I run with a running group every Saturday, then we stop after for a coffee or smoothie bowl, or something fun after our run. For me, when I'm with friends and exercising and moving, that is complete rejuvenation. Sometimes it is going to bed early and reading a good book. Sometimes it is sitting on my front porch with a coffee, enjoying the fresh air. Sometimes it is walking my dog with my husband.

When I remember to take care of myself, it helps me to manage small doses of stress and stay relatively calm.

ACTION PLAN:

Rejuvenate Your Body:

- Get Moving
- Get Your Sleep

Notes:

_____

_____

_____

_____

_____

_____

_____

_____

5. Community and Fun

As we get older, sometimes we focus so much on our work and family, we let our friendships go astray, or lose connection as we don't have as much in common anymore. Having good friends has been key in helping me recover from stress. I found these friendships are one of the most amazing parts of my recovery. I get so much joy when I run with my friends. I look forward to Saturday mornings, and I don't even mind that I sometimes have to get up at 4:30 am! I am continually finding new friends that I have a common interest with, whether I find them on social media, in the neighborhood, or other moms and dads that I meet through my son.

Friendships help keep us healthy and find balance. I love going away with friends on girls' trips. Whether it is business or running trips to Disney, it is just so much fun, and it helps you to focus on what is really important in life. Feeling that you are part of a community, adding value, and having people there to laugh and cry with you, as well as have fun, is an important connection.

It is so easy to withdraw from life and become isolated and alone, only connecting with your immediate family. These connections are really important for your social brain which needs to connect with others on a regular basis.

ACTION PLAN:

Seek Community:

- Connect with Others
- Nurture Friendships
- Plan some fun!

Notes:

_____

_____

_____

_____

_____

_____

_____

_____

6. Managing Your Time

When you are a perfectionist, you are always watching the clock, at least I know that I was. So, one of the first things I decided to do years ago was that I took off my watch, and never wore it again. I felt I was tied to my watch, and letting it go was incredibly freeing for me.

I could never wear an Apple watch, it would drive me crazy having that on my arm, buzzing and lighting up all the time. It would be very distracting to me. It would take me away from being present in the moment.

I also cannot wear a fitness tracker, because as a perfectionist, if I didn't get in my 10,000 steps, I would start walking manically around my house with my husband asking me what I was doing. I seriously drove him crazy, and myself too! So, that fitness tracker sits in my drawer now.

I used to stress about my runs and my pace and finish times. As a perfectionist, you can be super competitive, even if it is with yourself! I let go of finish times and pace per minute - and I let in the joy of running. And that felt so good!

The lesson I have for you is this:

Know your limitations.

Know what triggers you.

Get rid of it.

I was the queen of "To Do" lists. I had lists of my lists. My husband groaned every time I took out a list and started rattling off all that we needed to do. One day, I decided to stop making lists. This is not always the best advice because obviously things need to get done, so it is about finding balance. Now on Sunday nights I sit down with my calendar, write out my schedule of appointments for the week and make a list of things that need to be done for the week. Then I break that down day by day and pick three things that absolutely need to be done that day and block time for those. Time blocking has helped me to focus and be stress free.

For example, if I have a project for work, I give myself an uninterrupted hour. I need to clean and do the laundry? I block a half hour of time. It helps me stay focused, and not get overwhelmed. It is a schedule, but it is not so rigid that it gets me making a to-do list for my to-do list.

Time blocking, or sprints, are allocating yourself a certain amount of time to do something and totally focusing on that. If you knew you had to get on a plane to another city at 5:00 pm, and all of your daily tasks had to get done before you got on that plane, they would get done because you had a deadline. You have to get on the plane, so then you can't do them anymore. If that plane ride was in seven days' time, all of those tasks would probably expand to fit those extra seven days.

Setting a deadline, a time block, or a sprint encourages you to do what you need to do now and fit it into that time you've got rather than having all of your tasks expand to fit whatever time you have. You can start with as little as 10 minutes to get something done.

ACTION PLAN:

Manage Your Time;

- Pick 3 things to do each day
- Time block
- Set realistic deadlines

Notes:

_____

_____

_____

_____

_____

_____

_____

_____

7. Ask For Help

Asking for help can be daunting and scary, but it can also be the most freeing thing you can do for yourself. If you are overwhelmed by your life, ask for help from your family. If you are struggling mentally or physically, ask your health care provider for help.

I recently read a book called The Boy, the Mole, the Fox and the Horse, by Charlie Mackesy, and loved this amazing quote from the book. "Asking for help isn't giving up," said the horse. "It's refusing to give up."

Some people think asking for help is weak, but really it is a strong thing to do, because you are putting your mental and physical health first. It will help to you help your family, because once you ask for help, you can make the changes you desire, to live the life you deserve, and the purpose you are here for.

There are all sorts of places you can ask for help. Your friends and family would probably love to help you out, and really enjoy contributing to your life in a positive way. Asking for help is strong because you are telling people precisely what itch you need scratching, and precisely what to do to help you.

I went through a really difficult time a few years ago and came out the other side. I asked for help, started doing these practices, and all these amazing things started happening in my life. Now, I am reaching back and helping other women with wellness and balance. I have written this book! I enjoy every single day. My health has never been better, and have no anxiety or depression at all, they have been replaced with hope.

If you are going through a difficult time, there is hope things can get better. When you put in the work, which are pretty simple steps and practices you can start every day, there is hope for joy. There is hope for you to live the life you are supposed to in a beautiful and enjoyable way.

ACTION PLAN:

Seek Help

- Talk to a family member
- Talk to a friend
- Reach out to a professional

Notes:

_____

_____

_____

_____

_____

_____

_____

_____

CHAPTER SEVENTEEN

How to get more help

My mission is to help you feel better about yourself, and to help you let go of perfectionism, so that you can start the recovery process, to start to heal, and be able to dream again. I run multiple courses, and I also offer group and individual coaching programs to help you.

Please reach out to your health care provider, a family member, friend, pastor, or confidant if you need someone to talk to. There is no shame in asking for help.

If you are not feeling safe, please call the National Suicide Hotline at 800-273-8255.

Here are some ways that I can help:

If you want to put this book into action, bit by bit, here is the link to my signature course to get you living the life you desire:

Letting Go of Perfection with Sheri
www.letgowithsheri.com

Scan This QR code to take you to the most up to date resources by Sheri

I also offer the following coaching and courses:

Transform Your Life with Private Coaching from Sheri
www.coachsheripoyant.com

Jumpstart Your Nutrition with Sheri Course
www.5weekjumpstart.com

Join my free FB Community where my husband Matt and I help families to live differently. We help families find balance in relationships, health and work so they can live out their true purpose.

www.jointhepoyants.com

If you know a perfectionist and want to help them, please give them a copy of this book.

FREEBIES

If you would like a free set of affirmation cards found in this book:
www.affirmationswithsheri.com

Feeling stress and want to change that will some fun and healthy smoothies? Grab my free smoothie recipe book here!

www.gettherecipes.com

Find me on the web:

Website www.sheripoyant.com

Facebook @sheripoyant
Instagram @sheripoyant
Twitter @sheripoyant

Subscribe to my YouTube Channel here…
www.thepoyantsyoutube.com

CPSIA information can be obtained
at www.ICGtesting.com
Printed in the USA
BVHW071944170821
614612BV00011B/850